Tony Berlant
New Terrain

Foreword © 2004 Kimberly Davis
ISBN 0-9708187-2-6

Tony Berlant
New Terrain

L | A | LOUVER

Out of Bounds, 2002
Found and fabricated printed tin
collaged on plywood with steel brads
72 x 48 inches [182.9 x 121.9 cm]

Collection of Bradley Bayou and
Mark Allen Itkin

When Tony Berlant was a child, his family spent a good deal of time exploring the desert around Palm Springs. Occasionally they would continue driving until they found themselves in Arizona, a place of wonderment: the Grand Canyon, the Meteorite Crater, the Petrified Forest, and Native Americans living in a largely traditional way. These childhood excursions influenced Berlant greatly, and his fascination with the area inspired him to become a collector of southwest Native American art—including Navajo blankets, prehistoric ceramics and kachinas. These objects are geometrized depictions of their world, and they helped shape how Berlant developed his own work. There are other artists who have influenced him over the years, including Bosch, Courbet, Cézanne, Monet, Picasso, Cornell, de Kooning and Diebenkorn, who along with the Native Americans, are his chosen ancestors. More recently Berlant has focused on collecting early-man tools, some of which are worked stones over a million years old. The experience of holding and examining the stones brings him into a hand-to-hand contact with his genetic roots, and with the spirit of the rocks from which they were made.

Berlant has continued to visit the desert, just a few hours from his studio. The end of the city and the edge of the desert is a symbolic dividing line between the rational and the subjective, the known and the unknown, the conscious and the subconscious. Everything in that zone is filled with pattern, order, and multiple layers of meaning. Berlant has observed that this landscape allows him to experience intense and vibrant associations, which he perceives as a transparent screen hanging between nature and himself. He aims to make these feelings and images visible in his work, considering them more *mindscape* than landscape. Paradoxically, the works present a world that is without people, yet is filled with human presence. By attempting to make more-or-less representational images through his technique of collaging found and fabricated printed tin onto wood panels, Berlant creates visions and connections that have a life of their own.

Kimberly Davis
Venice, CA
March 2004

A Rare Sighting, 2003
Found and fabricated printed tin
collaged on plywood with steel brads
40 x 66 inches [101.6 x 167.6 cm]

Collection of Bruce and Aulana Peters

Joshua Tree, 2001
Found and fabricated printed tin collaged on plywood with steel brads
36 x 174 inches [91.4 x 442 cm]

Collection of Dr. Lauren L. Reager

Rio, 2001
Found and fabricated printed tin collaged on plywood with steel brads
114 x 96 inches [290 x 243.8 cm]

Collection of the Artist

Looking Towards Hopi, 2002
Found and fabricated printed tin collaged on plywood with steel brads
48 x 72 inches [121.9 x 182.9 cm]

Collection of Hope Warschaw and John Law

What You See Is Who You Are, 2002-2003
Found and fabricated printed tin collaged on plywood with steel brads
10 x 58 feet [3.1 x 17.7 meters]

Collection of Target Corporation, Minneapolis, Minnesota

A Chance Encounter, 2003
Found and fabricated printed tin collaged on plywood with steel brads
60 x 48 inches [152.4 x 121.9 cm]

Collection of Rick and Helen Zeff

Painted Desert, 2001
Found and fabricated printed tin collaged on plywood with steel brads
48 x 216 inches [121.9 x 548.6 cm]

Collection of Dallas Price-Van Breda

Friday Harbor, 2003
Found and fabricated printed tin collaged on plywood with steel brads
96 x 108 inches [243.8 x 274.3 cm]

Private Collection

Savannah, 2003
Found and fabricated printed tin collaged on plywood with steel brads
48 x 60 inches [121.9 x 152.4 cm]

Topanga, 2001
Found and fabricated printed tin collaged on plywood with steel brads
96 x 132 inches [243.8 x 335.3 cm]

Collection of Alexander and Nancy Furlotti

Coat of Many Colors, 2002
Found and fabricated printed tin collaged on plywood with steel brads
49 x 61 inches [124.5 x 154.9 cm]

Private Collection

New Terrain
22 April–22 May, 2004

page 29

Indian Wells, 2004
Found and fabricated printed tin collaged on plywood with steel brads
34 x 36 inches [86.4 x 91.4 cm]

Morongo, 2004
Found and fabricated printed tin collaged on plywood with steel brads
48 x 72 inches [121.9 x 182.9 cm]

Nocturne, 2004
Found and fabricated printed tin collaged on plywood with steel brads
48 x 36 inches [121.9 x 91.4 cm]

Distant Memory, 2004
Found and fabricated printed tin collaged on plywood with steel brads
28 x 28 inches [71.1 x 71.1 cm]

pages 36–37

Yesterday, Today, and Tomorrow, 2004
Found and fabricated printed tin collaged on plywood with steel brads
36 x 84 inches [91.4 x 213.4 cm]

Divina Muse, 2002
Found and fabricated printed tin collaged on plywood with steel brads
78 x 48 inches [198.1 x 121.9 cm]

Zona Rosa, 2004
Found and fabricated printed tin collaged on plywood with steel brads
30 x 30 inches [76.2 x 76.2 cm]

Full Court, 2004
Found and fabricated printed tin
collaged on plywood with steel brads
46 x 77 inches [116.8 x 195.6 cm]

Virgin Ground, 2003
Found and fabricated printed tin collaged on plywood with steel brads
36 x 48 inches [91.4 x 121.9 cm]

Ground, 2004
Found and fabricated printed tin collaged on plywood with steel brads
42 1/16 x 62 1/2 inches [106.8 x 158.7 cm]

Untitled Romance, 2004
Found and fabricated printed tin collaged on plywood with steel brads
24 ½ x 32 inches [62.2 x 81.3 cm]

New Terrain, 2004
Found and fabricated printed tin
collaged on plywood with steel brads
46 x 77 inches [116.8 x 195.6 cm]

Star Garden, 2004
Found and fabricated printed tin collaged on plywood with steel brads
36 x 48 ½ inches [91.4 x 123.2 cm]

pages 54–55

Within, 2004
Found and fabricated printed tin collaged on plywood with steel brads
28 x 66 inches [71.1 x 167.6 cm]

Indian Wells, 2004
Found and fabricated printed tin
collaged on plywood with steel brads
34 x 36 inches [86.4 x 91.4 cm]
page 29

Morongo, 2004
Found and fabricated printed tin
collaged on plywood with steel brads
48 x 72 inches [121.9 x 182.9 cm]
pages 30–31

Nocturne, 2004
Found and fabricated printed tin
collaged on plywood with steel brads
48 x 36 inches [121.9 x 91.4 cm]
page 32

Distant Memory, 2004
Found and fabricated printed tin
collaged on plywood with steel brads
28 x 28 inches [71.1 x 71.1 cm]
page 35

Yesterday, Today, and Tomorrow, 2004
Found and fabricated printed tin
collaged on plywood with steel brads
36 x 84 inches [91.4 x 213.4 cm]
pages 36–37

Divina Muse, 2002
Found and fabricated printed tin
collaged on plywood with steel brads
78 x 48 inches [198.1 x 121.9 cm]
page 39

Zona Rosa, 2004
Found and fabricated printed tin
collaged on plywood with steel brads
30 x 30 inches [76.2 x 76.2 cm]
page 40

Full Court, 2004
Found and fabricated printed tin
collaged on plywood with steel brads
46 x 77 inches [116.8 x 195.6 cm]
page 42–43

Virgin Ground, 2003
Found and fabricated printed tin
collaged on plywood with steel brads
36 x 48 inches [91.4 x 121.9 cm]
page 45

Ground, 2004
Found and fabricated printed tin
collaged on plywood with steel brads
42 $\frac{1}{16}$ x 62 $\frac{1}{2}$ inches [106.8 x 158.7 cm]
page 46–47

Untitled Romance, 2004
Found and fabricated printed tin
collaged on plywood with steel brads
24 $\frac{1}{2}$ x 32 inches [62.2 x 81.3 cm]
page 48

New Terrain, 2004
Found and fabricated printed tin
collaged on plywood with steel brads
46 x 77 inches [116.8 x 195.6 cm]
pages 50–51

Star Garden, 2004
Found and fabricated printed tin
collaged on plywood with steel brads
36 x 48 $\frac{1}{2}$ inches [91.4 x 123.2 cm]
page 53

Within, 2004
Found and fabricated printed tin
collaged on plywood with steel brads
28 x 66 inches [71.1 x 167.6 cm]
pages 54–55

Tony Berlant

Born August 7, 1941 in New York City, New York

Education

1961 University of California, Los Angeles, BA, Summa Cum Laude
1962 University of California, Los Angeles, MA
1963 University of California, Los Angeles, MFA

Research Affiliate, Peabody Museum of Archaeology and Ethnology,
Harvard University, Cambridge, MA, 2001–present

Lives in Santa Monica, California

Commissions:

2003	Target Corporation, Minneapolis, Minnesota
1999	Junipero Serra State Office Building, Los Angeles, California
1998	Wilshire Boulevard Temple, Los Angeles, California
1997	Twentieth Century Fox Film Corporation, FBC Operations Building Lobby, Los Angeles, California
1996	U.S. Federal Building and Courthouse, Sacramento, California
1994	Faret Tachikawa Art Park, Tokyo, Japan
	Washington National Airport, Washington, D.C.
1992	Palm Springs Convention Center, Palm Springs, California
1991	The Minneapolis Institute of Arts, Minneapolis, Minnesota
1990	Fashion Institute of Design and Marketing, Los Angeles, California
1988	The Contemporary Art Museum, Honolulu, Hawaii
	California Arts Council, Department of Motor Vehicles, Davis
1987	San Francisco International Airport, San Francisco, California
1986	Xavier Fourcade, Inc., New York, New York
	Rebecca's Restaurant, Venice, California

Public Collections:

Arizona State University Art Museum, Tempe, Arizona
Art Institute of Chicago, Chicago, Illinois
Fort Worth Museum of Contemporary Art, Forth Worth, Texas
Hirshhorn Museum and Sculpture Garden, Smithsonian Institution, Washington, D.C.
La Jolla Museum of Contemporary Art, La Jolla, California
Long Beach Museum of Art, Long Beach, California
Los Angeles County Museum of Art, Los Angeles, California
Museum of Contemporary Art, Los Angeles, California
Oakland Museum, Oakland, California
North Carolina Museum of Art, Raleigh, North Carolina
Palm Springs Desert Museum, Palm Springs, California
Philadelphia Museum of Art, Philadelphia, Pennsylvania
Phoenix Art Museum, Phoenix, Arizona
San Francisco Museum of Modern Art, San Francisco, California
Sheldon Memorial Art Gallery, Lincoln, Nebraska
Skirball Cultural Center, Los Angeles, California
Wichita Art Museum, Wichita, Kansas
Whitney Museum of American Art, New York, New York
Yale University Art Museum, New Haven, Connecticut

Photography:
Brian Forrest
Robert Wedemeyer

On the cover:
Ground (detail), 2004
Found and fabricated printed tin collaged on plywood with steel brads
42 $\frac{1}{16}$ x 62 $\frac{1}{2}$ inches [106.8 x 158.7 cm]

Inside cover:
Ground (detail), 2004
Found and fabricated printed tin collaged on plywood with steel brads
42 $\frac{1}{16}$ x 62 $\frac{1}{2}$ inches [106.8 x 158.7 cm]

Designed by Gregg Einhorn in Santa Monica
with Tony Berlant, Peter Goulds, Liz Fischbach and Izabela Jadach at L.A. Louver.

Printed and bound by S & P Printers

With thanks to Rae Lewis from Tony Berlant's studio and the staff at L.A. Louver.

A list of all L.A. Louver catalogues can be obtained from the gallery.

Published by L.A. Louver on the occasion of the exhibition
Tony Berlant: New Terrain
22 April–22 May, 2004

L.A. Louver
45 North Venice Boulevard
Venice, California 90291

tel 310.822.4955 fax 310.821.7529
info@lalouver.com
www.lalouver.com

Hours
Tuesday–Saturday 10am–6pm
Monday by appointment